Table of Contents

Introduction

With over 50 million inhabitants Colombia is one of the most ethnically and linguistically diverse countries in the world, with its rich cultural heritage reflecting influences by various Amerindian civilizations, European settlement, forced African labor, and immigration from Europe and the greater Middle East. Urban centres are concentrated in the Andean highlands and the Caribbean coast.

Colombia has been inhabited by various indigenous peoples since at least 12,000 BCE, including the Muisca, Quimbaya, and the Tairona. The Spanish landed first in La Guajira in 1499 and by the mid-16th century annexed part of the region, establishing the New Kingdom of Granada, with Santafé de Bogotá as its capital. Independence from Spain was achieved in 1810, with what is now Colombia emerging as the United Provinces of New Granada. The new nation experimented with federalism as the Granadine Confederation (1858), and then the United States of Colombia (1863), before the Republic of Colombia was finally declared in 1886. Panama seceded in 1903, leading to Colombia's present borders.

Beginning in the 1960s, the country suffered from an asymmetric low-intensity armed conflict and political violence, both of which escalated in the 1990s. Since 2005, there has been significant improvement in security, stability, and rule of law, as well as unprecedented economic growth and development.

Colombia is one of the world's 17 megadiverse countries and has the second-highest level of biodiversity in the world. Its territory encompasses Amazon rainforest, highlands, grasslands, and deserts, and it is the only country in South America with coastlines and islands along both the Atlantic and Pacific.

Colombia is considered a regional actor in international affairs, being the only NATO Global Partner in Latin America and a member of several major global and regional institutions, including the OECD, the UN, the World Trade Organization, the OAS, the Pacific Alliance, the Association of Caribbean States, an associate member of Mercosur and other international organizations. Colombia's diversified economy is the third largest in South America, with macroeconomic stability and favorable long-term growth prospects. It is subsequently classified as part of the CIVETS group of leading emerging markets.

Owing to its location, the present territory of Colombia was a corridor of early human civilization from Mesoamerica and the Caribbean to the Andes and Amazon basin. The oldest archaeological finds are from the Pubenza and El Totumo sites in the Magdalena Valley 100 kilometres (62 mi) southwest of Bogotá. These sites date from the Paleoindian period (18,000–8000 BCE). At Puerto Hormiga and other sites, traces from the Archaic Period (~8000–2000 BCE) have been found. Vestiges indicate that there was also early occupation in the regions of El Abra and Tequendama in Cundinamarca. The oldest pottery discovered in the Americas, found at San Jacinto, dates to 5000–4000 BCE.

Indigenous people inhabited the territory that is now Colombia by 12,500 BCE. Nomadic hunter-gatherer tribes at the El Abra, Tibitó and Tequendama sites near present-day Bogotá traded with one another and with other cultures from the Magdalena River Valley. A site including eight miles of pictographs that is under study at Serranía de la Lindosa was revealed in November 2020. Their age is suggested as being 12,500 years old (c. 10,480 B.C.) by the anthropologists working on the site because of extinct fauna depicted. That would have been during the earliest known human occupation of the area now known as Colombia.

Between 5000 and 1000 BCE, hunter-gatherer tribes transitioned to agrarian societies; fixed settlements were established, and pottery appeared. Beginning in the 1st millennium BCE, groups of Amerindians including the Muisca, Zenú, Quimbaya, and Tairona developed the political system of cacicazgos with a pyramidal structure of power headed by caciques. The Muisca inhabited mainly the area of what is now the Departments of Boyacá and Cundinamarca high plateau (Altiplano Cundiboyacense) where they formed the Muisca Confederation. They farmed maize, potato, quinoa, and cotton, and traded gold, emeralds, blankets, ceramic handicrafts, coca and especially rock salt with neighboring nations. The Tairona inhabited northern Colombia in the isolated mountain range of Sierra Nevada de

Santa Marta. The Quimbaya inhabited regions of the Cauca River Valley between the Western and Central Ranges of the Colombian Andes. Most of the Amerindians practiced agriculture and the social structure of each indigenous community was different. Some groups of indigenous people such as the Caribs lived in a state of permanent war, but others had less bellicose attitudes.

Independence

Since the beginning of the periods of conquest and colonization, there were several rebel movements against Spanish rule, but most were either crushed or remained too weak to change the overall situation. The last one that sought outright independence from Spain sprang up around 1810 and culminated in the Colombian Declaration of Independence, issued on 20 July 1810, the day that is now celebrated as the nation's Independence Day. This movement followed the independence of St. Domingue (present-day Haiti) in 1804, which provided some support to an eventual leader of this rebellion: Simón Bolívar. Francisco de Paula Santander also would play a decisive role.

A movement was initiated by Antonio Nariño, who opposed Spanish centralism and led the opposition against the Viceroyalty. Cartagena became independent in November 1811. In 1811 the United Provinces of New Granada were proclaimed, headed by Camilo Torres Tenorio. The emergence of two distinct ideological currents among the patriots (federalism and centralism) gave rise to a period of instability. Shortly after the Napoleonic Wars ended, Ferdinand VII, recently restored to the throne in Spain, unexpectedly decided to send military forces to retake most of northern South America. The viceroyalty was restored under the command of Juan Sámano, whose regime punished those who participated in the patriotic movements, ignoring the political nuances of the juntas. The retribution stoked renewed rebellion, which, combined with a weakened Spain, made possible a successful rebellion led by the Venezuelan-born Simón Bolívar, who finally proclaimed independence in

1819. The pro-Spanish resistance was defeated in 1822 in the present territory of Colombia and in 1823 in Venezuela.

The territory of the Viceroyalty of New Granada became the Republic of Colombia, organized as a union of the current territories of Colombia, Panama, Ecuador, Venezuela, parts of Guyana and Brazil and north of Marañón River. The Congress of Cúcuta in 1821 adopted a constitution for the new Republic. Simón Bolívar became the first President of Colombia, and Francisco de Paula Santander was made Vice President. However, the new republic was unstable and three countries emerged from the collapse of Gran Colombia in 1830 (New Granada, Ecuador and Venezuela).

Colombia lies at the crossroads of Latin America and the broader American continent, and as such has been hit by a wide range of cultural influences. Native American, Spanish and other European, African, American, Caribbean, and Middle Eastern influences, as well as other Latin American cultural influences, are all present in Colombia's modern culture. Urban migration, industrialization, globalization, and other political, social and economic changes have also left an impression.

Many national symbols, both objects and themes, have arisen from Colombia's diverse cultural traditions and aim to represent what Colombia, and the Colombian people, have in common. Cultural expressions in Colombia are promoted by the government through the Ministry of Culture.

Cuisine

Colombia's varied cuisine is influenced by its diverse fauna and flora as well as the cultural traditions of the ethnic groups. Colombian dishes and ingredients vary widely by region. Some of the most common ingredients are: cereals such as rice and maize; tubers such as potato and cassava; assorted legumes; meats, including beef, chicken, pork and goat; fish; and seafood. Colombia cuisine also features a variety of tropical fruits such as cape gooseberry, feijoa, arazá, dragon fruit, mangostino, granadilla, papaya, guava, mora (blackberry), lulo, soursop and passionfruit. Colombia is one of the world's largest consumers of fruit juices.

11

Among the most representative appetizers and soups are patacones (fried green plantains), sancocho de gallina (chicken soup with root vegetables) and ajiaco (potato and corn soup). Representative snacks and breads are pandebono, arepas (corn cakes), aborrajados (fried sweet plantains with cheese), torta de choclo, empanadas and almojábanas. Representative main courses are bandeja paisa, lechona tolimense, mamona, tamales and fish dishes (such as arroz de lisa), especially in coastal regions where kibbeh, suero, costeño cheese and carimañolas are also eaten. Representative side dishes are papas chorreadas (potatoes with cheese), remolachas rellenas con huevo duro (beets stuffed with hard-boiled egg) and arroz con coco (coconut rice). Organic food is a current trend in big cities, although in general across the country the fruits and veggies are very natural and fresh.

Representative desserts are buñuelos, natillas, Maria Luisa cake, bocadillo made of guayaba (guava jelly), cocadas (coconut balls), casquitos de guayaba (candied guava peels), torta de natas, obleas, flan de mango, roscón, milhoja, manjar blanco, dulce de feijoa, dulce de papayuela, torta de mojicón, and esponjado de curuba. Typical sauces (salsas) are hogao (tomato and onion sauce) and Colombian-style ají.

Some representative beverages are coffee (Tinto), champús, cholado, lulada, avena colombiana, sugarcane juice, aguapanela, aguardiente, hot chocolate and fresh fruit juices (often made with water or milk).

Colombian Arepas

This is a quick and easy recipe to make delicious Colombian arepas. They are usually served for breakfast, as a side dish, or even for a quick meal.

Ingredients

- 1 cup warm water
- 1 cup pre-cooked white corn meal (such as P.A.N.®)
- 1 cup shredded mozzarella cheese
- 1 tablespoon butter
- ½ teaspoon salt, or to taste
- cooking spray

Directions

Step 1

Mix water, corn meal, mozzarella cheese, butter, and salt together in a large bowl. Knead until mixed well and the dough has a soft consistency. Form balls the size of a medium orange and place them between 2 sheets of plastic wrap. Flatten with a rolling pin to your desired thickness.

Step 2

Cut the dough into circles using a cereal bowl or drinking glass, lip-down, through the plastic wrap. Remove the plastic wrap and remove excess dough.

Step 3

Coat a griddle with cooking spray and heat to medium-high. Add arepas and grill until golden brown, about 5 minutes per side. Serve immediately.

Cook's Note:

If the dough is too dry, add a little bit more water. If it's too moist, add more corn flour.

Nutrition Facts

Per Serving:

125 calories; protein 5.8g; carbohydrates 13.9g; fat 5.2g; cholesterol 17.1mg; sodium 325.2mg.

Top 12 Colombian Foods and Dishes You Must Try

Empanadas: These wonderful empanadas are one of the most popular Colombian snacks. The crust is made with corn masa while the filling is made with meat, potatoes and spices. It's traditional to serve these empanadas with ají (Colombian-style hot sauce).

2. Picada o Fritanga: There are different variations of this dish and every cook adds different ingredients to their platter, but some of the most popular ingredients in the Piacda Colombiana are fried green plantains (patacones), pork belly (chicharrón), small yellow potatoes (papa criolla), chorizo, pork ribs, yuca fries (yuca frita), morcilla and ripe plantains.

3. Bandeja Paisa: This is probably the most popular Colombian dish, originally from the Andean region of the country where the people are called "Paisas" and the area where I was born and raised.

4. Ajiaco: It's a hearty soup from the capital of the country, Bogotá, and is made with chicken, three varieties of potatoes, corn and guascas. Ajiaco is usually served with cream, capers, ají and avocado. It's comfort in a bowl!

5. Sancocho Trifásico: This is very thick soup made with root vegetables and different kinds of meats, in a broth, usually

flavored with herbs, onions, garlic and peppers. The perfect Sunday meal!

6. Cazuela de Mariscos: This is a seafood stew from the Atantic Coast of Colombia made with a broth from with coconut milk, vegetables, spices and different kind of seafood. It's creamy, rich and very comforting.

7. Refajo: This is a popular and refreshing Colombian cocktail made with beer and "Colombiana", a popular Colombian soda. It 's the perfect summer drink.

8. Chocolate con Queso: Hot chocolate with cheese is a very popular drink and perfect for the cold weather. It's usually served for breakfast or an afternoon snack in the Andean region of Colombia. The combiantion of chocolate with cheese may sound weird to you, but it's absolutely amazing.

9. Tajadas de Plátano: Ripe plantain fritters are one of the most popular side dishes in Colombia and very simple to make.

8. Patacones: Also known as tostones, patacones are a popular Colombian appetizer or side dish made green plantains.

9. Arroz con Coco Titoté: This coconut rice is a traditional recipe from the Caribbean region of Colombia. Arroz con coco is the perfect side dish for seafood.

10. Pandebono: These are small, baked, cheese bread rolls, perfect for breakfast or an afternoon snack with hot chocolate or coffee.

11. Casado o Bocadillo con Queso: This is a simple and easy to make Colombian dessert. The combination of salty cheese and sweet guava paste is one of those heavenly combinations that you simply must try.

12. Torta Negra: There are many variations of this Colombian black cake throughout the country, every person and family having their own recipe, using different combinations of wine fruits and nuts in their cake.

Chicken and Rice (Arroz con Pollo)

Ingredients

(4 Servings)

Chicken and Stock

- 2 whole chicken breast, bone in and skin removed
- 1 scallion
- ½ white onion
- 2 garlic cloves
- ½ tablespoon ground cumin
- ½ tablespoon sazon Goya with azafran
- 1 bay leaf
- Salt and Pepper

Rice

- 2 tablespoons olive oil
- ¼ cup chopped onion
- 1 garlic clove, minced
- ¼ cup chopped red bell pepper

- ¼ cup chopped green pepper
- 1 cup long- grain white rice
- 1 tablespoon tomato paste
- 1 chicken bouillon tablet
- 2 ½ cups chicken stock
- ½ tablespoon sazon goya with azafran
- ¼ cup chopped fresh cilantro
- ½ cup frozen peas
- ½ cup frozen diced carrots
- ½ cup frozen diced green beans

Directions

1. Place the chicken breast, 5 cups water and the remaining ingredients for the stock in a medium pot. Bring to a boil, cover and reduce the heat to medium low. Cook for 20 to 25 minutes. Turn the heat off and let the chicken rest in the pot for about 15 minutes covered. Let it cool, shred and set aside. Strain stock and measure 2 ½ cups and set aside.

2. In a medium pot, heat the olive oil over medium-high heat. Add the onions, green peppers, garlic and red bell pepper. Cook until the onions are translucent, about 4 to 5 minutes.

3. Add the rice, tomato paste, chicken bouillon and sazon goya. Stir until the rice is well coated about 3 minutes. Add the chicken stock and bring to a boil. Then reduce the heat to low. Cover and simmer for about 15 minutes. Add the peas, carrots and green beans and cook for and additional 7 minutes, add the shredded chicken and cilantro, mix well with a fork, cover and cook for 5 minutes more.

4. Serve and Enjoy!

Ají Llanero (Los Llanos Orientales Hot Sauce)

Ají Llanero is a traditional hot sauce from Los Llanos Orientales (The Eastern Plains) in Colombia. It's located east of the Colombian Andes and north of the Amazon, and is shared between Colombia and Venezuela.

Los Llanos are the home of the Colombian llaneros (cowboys) and where the primary economic activity is the herding of cattle, which explains why this region of the country is known for their delicious beef recipes. The most recognized dish In Los Llanos is the Veal a la Llanera, served with yuca and plantain.

This Ají Llanero is also known in Colombia as Ají Llanero de Leche, Ají Pique Llanero, and Ajicero, or Picante Andino in Venezuela. There are different versions of this hot sauce depending on the family, cook and country. Some people add cumin, oil, onions, oregano, and more. The recipe I am sharing is very simple and traditional, but you can add more ingredients to your taste. It's served typically with soups and stews, but it's also delicious over grilled meats, fish and vegetables.

Ingredients:

- 1 red pepper, chopped
- 1/2 habanero or ají pique, chopped
- 1 garlic clove, chopped

- 1 1/2 cups warm milk
- 2 tablespoons chopped scallions
- 1 tablespoon cilantro, chopped
- Salt and pepper to you taste

Instructions:

1. Mix all the ingredients well in a glass container.

2. Let rest for a minimum of 3 hours before using.

Bandeja Paisa (Paisa Platter)

Bandeja Paisa is probably the most popular Colombian dish, originally from the Andean region of the country where the people are called "Paisas" and the area where I was born and raised.

Bandeja paisa is something I've eaten all of my life and if I have to choose my last meal on this earth, this is the one. Tradionally, Bandeja paisa includes beans, white rice, chicharrón, carne en polvo, chorizo, fried egg, ripe plantain, avocado and arepa, but you can substitute the powdered beef for grilled beef or pork. I usually make the beans and powdered beef the day before to make it easier.

Ingredients

(4 Servings)

- 1 Recipe Paisa Pinto Beans (Frijoles Paisas)
- 1 Recipe white Rice (Arroz Blanco)
- 1 Recipe Powdered Beef (Carne en Polvo)
- 4 Fried Pork Belly (Chicharrones)
- 4 Cooked Chorizos
- 4 Fried eggs sunny side up
- 4 baked plantainsor Tajadas de Plátano
- 1 Recipe Hogao
- Lime and Avocado for Serving

Directions

1. Prepare the beans, hogao and powdered beef one day ahead and keep in the refrigerator.

2. When you are going to serve the bandeja paisa, heat the beans and powdered beefand hogao. Make the chicharrones.

3. Cook the white rice and plantains.

4. Fry the eggs and chorizos.

5. To serve, place the rice in a tray or platter and place the rest of the ingredients as you like. I prefer the beans in a separate bowl, but you can ladle the beans next to the rice if you like.

6. Bring the hogao in a serving dish to the table, so people can place it on top of the beans if they like. Enjoy!

Colombian Empanadas (Empanadas Colombianas)

These Colombian Empanadas are a popular snack in Colombia and are served by most Colombian restaurants in the USA. Traditionally, these delicious fritters are made with shredded pork and beef, but in my family we always make them with ground meat. Serve them with ají and lime wedges on the side.

In Colombia, empanadas are also sold outside of the churches. They are usually small and just have potato filling, a great alternative for vegetarians and absolutely delicious.

For the vegetarian version of this Colombian Empanadas recipe, follow all the instructions and just omitting the beef and pork.

Ingredients:

(About Twenty, 3 inch empanadas)

- Vegetable oil for frying
- Lime and ají for serving

Dough or Masa:

- 1 ½ cups precooked yellow cornmeal (masarepa)
- 2 cups water
- 1 tablespoon vegetable oil

- ½ tablespoon sazon Goya with azafran
- ½ teaspoon Salt

Filling:

- 2 cups peeled and diced white potatoes
- 1 chicken or vegetable bouillon tablet
- 1 tablespoon olive oil
- ¼ cup chopped white onions
- 1 cup chopped tomato
- ½ teaspoon salt
- ¼ cup chopped green onions
- 1 chopped garlic clove
- 2 tablespoon chopped fresh cilantro
- 2 tablespoon chopped red bell pepper
- ¼ teaspoon black pepper
- ½ pound ground pork and beef

Directions

1. To prepare the dough:Place the masarepa in a large bowl. Add the sazon Goya and salt and stir to mix well. Add the water and oil and mix to form dough. Pat the dough into a ball and knead for 2 minutes or until smooth. Cover with plastic and set aside for 20 minutes.

2. Meanwhile, to make the filling, cook the potatoes in a pot with water and the bouillon tablet for 20-25 minutes or until tender. Drain and gently mash the potatoes. Set aside.

3. Heat 1 tablespoon olive oil in a large, heavy skillet. Add the onion and cook over medium-low heat stirring frequently, for 5 minutes. Add the tomatoes, green onions, garlic, bell pepper, cilantro, salt and black pepper. Cook for about 15 minutes.

4. Add the ground pork and beef. Cook, breaking up the meat with a wooden spoon, for 10 to 15 minutes or until the mixture is fairly dry.

5. Transfer the meat mixture to the mashed potatoes bowl and mix well to combine.

6. Break small portions of the dough, about 1 ½ tablespoons each one, and form each portion into a ball by rolling between the palms of your hands.

7. Place the balls of dough between two pieces of plastic and roll each out very thinly to form a circle. Remove the top plastic and place 1 tablespoon of the filling in the center of each.

8. Then using the plastic underneath, fold the dough over to enclose the filling, forming a half circle. Tightly seal the edges by crimping with the tines of a fork.

9. Fill a large pot with vegetable oil and heat over medium heat to 360° F.

10. Carefully place 3 or 4 empanadas at the time in the heated oil and fry for about 2 minutes until golden on all sides.

11. Using a slotted spoon transfer the empanadas to a plate lined with paper towels. Serve with ají and lime on the side.

Pandebono (Colombian Cheese bread)

Ingredients

- (12 pandebonos)
- 2/3 cup cassava starch or yuca flour
- 1/4 cup precooked cornmeal or masarepa
- 1 cup Mexican queso freso or Colombian quesito
- 1 1/4 cup feta cheese
- 1 large egg

Directions

1. Pre-heat the oven to 400°F.
2. In a food processor, place the yuca flour, cheese and masarepa. Process until well combined. Add the egg slowly while food processor is running.
3. Divide the mixture into 12 equal size portions, shaping them into balls.
4. Place on a baking sheet lined with parchment paper and bake for about 15 to 20 minutes or until golden on top. Serve warm.

Colombian Hot Dogs (Perro Caliente Colombiano)

Medellin, like other cities in the world, has hot dogs stands on the streets and this recipe is very popular with them. In Colombia we don't grill the hotdogs or salchichas, we boil them and the toppings include coleslaw, pineapple sauce, ketchup, mayonnaise, mustard and potato chips. When my friends and I would go out to dance, we would usually end up at one of the best hot dog stands located on Poblado Avenue in Medellin at 2 o' clock in the morning. I really miss those times.

Ingredients:

For the pineapple Sauce (About 1 Cup)

- 2 cups fresh pineapple, peeled and cut into chunks
- 1/3 cup water
- 2 ½ tablespoons sugar or taste
- 1 ¼ teaspoon cornstarch
- Juice of ½ a lime

Ingredients Hot Dogs

- 6 hot dogs buns
- 6 pork and beef hot dogs or veggie dogs
- 1 cup pineapple sauce
- 1 cup cole slaw
- 1 small bag potato chips, crushed into fine pieces
- Mayonnaise
- Ketchup
- Mustard

Directions

1. Put the pineapple and water in a blender and blend until smooth.
2. Press the pineapple mixture through a sieve into a small saucepan. Discard the pineapple on the sieve.
3. Place the saucepan with the pineapple mixture over medium-low heat and add the lime juice and sugar. Cook, stirring for about 15 minutes.

4. In a small bowl blend the cornstarch with 1 tablespoon of water and then stir the mixture into the pineapple sauce.

5. Bring slowly to a boil, stirring until the sauce thickens. Simmer gently for 4 minutes while stirring.

6. Let it cool and transfer to a serving bowl.

7. In a medium pot bring water to a boil. Add the hot dogs to the boiling water and cover. Cook about 7 minutes.

8. Remove and drain on paper towels.

9. Place the hot dogs in the buns and top with pineapple sauce, coleslaw, mayonnaise, mustard and ketchup, topped with crushed potato chips. Serve and enjoy!

Colombian Style Stuffed Potatoes (Papas Rellenas Colombianas)

Papas Rellenas are a popular Colombian food that we eat for breakfast or as a snack. You can serve these Colombian Stuffed Potatoes hot or cold and they are delicious with ají sauce. Colombians have different versions of Papas Rellenas.

Ingredients

(10 stuffed potatoes)

- Vegetable oil for frying
- 5 medium potatoes
- ¼ teaspoon salt
- Meat Filling:
- 1 tablespoon olive oil
- 1 cup chopped tomato
- 1/3 cup chopped onion
- 1/3 cup chopped scallions
- 1 garlic clove, minced
- ½ teaspoon ground cumin
- ½ teaspoon sazon Goya with azafran
- ¼ teaspoon salt
- ¼ teaspoon ground pepper
- ½ pound ground beef

For a vegetarian version:

Use the same ingredients in the meat filling except the beef and add 1 cup frozen carrots and peas.

Batter:

- 1 egg
- ¼ cup all-purpose flour
- Pinch salt
- ½ tablespoon sazon Goya with azafran
- ¼ cup milk

Directions

1. Peel the potatoes and cut them into chunks, put them in a medium pot and cover with water and ¼ teaspoon of salt.
2. Bring the potatoes to a boil over medium high heat, then reduce the heat to medium and cook until fork tender about 20 minutes.

3. Drain the potatoes and mash with a fork or masher and set aside.

4. Prepare the filling, in a large sauce pan, heat 1 tablespoon olive oil over medium heat and add the onion, tomato, scallions, garlic, cumin, azafran, pepper and salt. Cook for 5 minutes or until the onions are translucent, add the beef and cook stirring occasionally about 10 – 15 minutes. Set aside to cool.

5. In a medium bowl place all the batter ingredients and whisk until smooth and set aside.

6. Divide the potato mash into 10 equal sized portions, about 1/3 cup each, and form each portion into a ball by rolling between the palms of your hands. Flatten into patties and place 1 ½ tablespoons of the filling in the center of each one. Shape the potato mixture with the filling into balls to enclose the filling completely.

7. Fill a large heavy pot with vegetable oil and heat over medium-high heat to 360° F.

8. Dip the stuffed potato into the batter and carefully place them in the hot oil and fry for about 4 minutes or until golden, turning over halfway through. Remove

the potatoes from the oil using a slotted spoon and drain in a plate with paper towels. Transfer to a serving plate and serve with Ají.

Colombian Stewed Beef with Hogao and Crispy Corn Arepas

Ingredients

- 1 Pre Brands Chuck Roast, 10 minutes out of fridge and patted dry
- 1.5 tsp sea salt
- 1 28 oz. can of diced tomatoes
- 1 tbsp. cumin
- 2 tbsp. sunflower oil (or other high heat oil)
- 1 bunch scallions, chopped
- 1 garlic clove, minced
- 1/2 tsp. salt
- 1 tsp. cumin
- 1 12 oz. can fire roasted diced tomatoes
- 1 lime, juiced

- 1/4 c. cilantro, chopped and packed
- 1 tsp. red wine vinegar
- 2 c. Masa Harina (corn flour)
- 2 tsp. salt
- 3-3.5 c. warm water
- 1/2 cup sunflower oil

Instructions

1. Season chuck roast with sea salt and set inside the Instant Pot*.
2. Pour diced tomatoes and cumin on the roast.
3. Secure lid and set IP to 'Manual' and use the + or I buttons to set to 45. Set top valve to 'Seal'.
4. For the Hogao, heat oil in large skillet over medium heat and sauté scallions until soft. Add garlic, cumin, and salt and cook until fragrant.
5. Add fire roasted tomatoes, vinegar, and lime juice. Cook for a few minutes and then turn to low for 5 minutes.

6. Taste and season with more vinegar or salt. Keep warm to serve with the beef.

7. To make the Arepas, whisk salt and corn meal in large bowl. Make a well in the middle.

8. Add water to the well in two parts. Mix together with wooden spoon incorporating the water to the meal slowly. You may have to use a whisk if it gets too clumpy. As the dough thickens you can start to use your hands. Eventually it will be a soft ball of dough. It should not be sticky to the touch. If it's too dry add more warm water a tsp at a time. If it's too sticky or wet, add a bit more corn meal in sprinkles.

9. Keep cutting the dough in half until you have 10-12 small wedges. Form into round ball in your hands. Press them flat in your palms or between two piece of plastic wrap.

10. Heat sunflower oil in a large heavy bottomed pot, like a dutch oven, make sure it's large enough so the oil is only about 1/8 inch high. Bring to medium-high heat. Test the oil is hot enough by sprinkling a bit of water

on the surface. It should sizzle and not splatter. Adjust heat as needed.

11. Using a slotted spatula or spoon lower your corn cakes into the oil. When there is nice brown crust on one side, flip and cook the other side. Remove onto a paper towel to let cool. Repeat in 3-4 batches until finished.

12. When warm but cool enough to touch, open the arepas length-wise, like an english muffin. Doing this while warm makes it easier.

13. When roast is finished, let is release naturally by waiting for the numbers to read 'LH: 0:10' which mean it's on low heat for 10 minutes. Then turn the valve on top to release.

14. Slowly open the pot away from your face. Shred chuck in the pot with 4 forks. Mix the tomatoes, and chuck together. Taste and season with salt.

15. Stuff Arepas with Chuck, Hogao, and any other desired toppings. Serve warm!

Colombian Beef Stew (Carne Guisada)

Savory beef, tender potatoes, and a richly spiced sauce make this Colombian Beef Stew a new twist on an old classic. Topped with creamy avocado-cilantro sauce, this satisfying dinner will quickly become a family favorite!

INGREDIENTS

FOR THE CARNE GUISADA

- 2 tablespoons vegetable oil
- 1 1/4 pounds stew beef
- 3 cups chopped ripe tomatoes (about 4 tomatoes)
- 2 cups chopped yellow onion (about 2 medium onions)
- 4 tablespoons minced garlic
- 3/4 teaspoon ground cumin
- 1/2 teaspoon ground cayenne pepper
- 2 cups beef broth
- 1 tablespoons white vinegar
- 1 pound baby red potatoes, cut into uniform bite-sized pieces

FOR THE CREAMY AVOCADO-CILANTRO SAUCE

- 1/2 of a large, ripe avocado
- Juice of half of one lime
- 1/2 cup cilantro leaves and stems
- 1 scallion (green onion)
- 1/4 teaspoon salt
- 4 tablespoons extra virgin olive oil

INSTRUCTIONS

1. Heat the oil in a 5-quart or larger Dutch oven over medium-high heat. Once the oil is shimmering, add the beef in a single layer and let cook, undisturbed, until the meat is browned and releases easily from the bottom of the pan (3-5 minutes). Turn the beef and repeat process to brown on each side.

2. Add the tomatoes and onion to the pot. Toss well and use a wooden spoon to scrape the browned bits from the bottom of the pan. Add the garlic, cumin, and cayenne pepper and cook for 30 seconds. Pour the beef broth and vinegar into the pot and allow the

contents of the pot to come to a boil. Turn the heat down to low, cover, and simmer until the beef is tender (90-120 minutes).

3. Add the potatoes and cook, uncovered, over medium heat for 30-60 minutes until the potatoes are tender.

4. Meanwhile, prepare the creamy avocado-cilantro sauce by placing the avocado, lime juice, cilantro, scallion, and salt into the bowl of a small food processor or blender. Pulse a few times, then slowly add the olive oil and continue to process until creamy and smooth.

5. Serve the stew warm topped with the creamy avocado-cilantro sauce.

Easy Colombian Chicken Stew - Sudado De Pollo

Fragrant and brimming with flavor, this classic Colombian Chicken Stew continues to please.

Satisfy your comfort food cravings with this easy one-pot Sudado de Pollo meal of drumsticks, bell pepper, onions, and potatoes, simmered to tenderness in just minutes.

Colombian chicken stew - sudado de pollo in a white Dutch oven skillet on a white background.

Perfect for a quick wecknight family meal or a dinner party with friends, this hearty, healthy dinner never disappoints. We have also included Instant Pot instructions below.

This gluten-free and dairy-free dish uses primary pantry ingredients that are seasoned with Sazon Goya con Azafran and cooked to perfection.

What Is Sazon Goya Con Azafran?

It's an exceptional seasoning blend that creates the authentic flavors of Latin cuisine. It contains Mexican saffron, cumin, garlic, and turmeric. It's an aromatic ingredient that adds flavor and color, and it's essential for paellas, stews, and rice dishes.

Colombian cuisine is influenced by Indigenous Colombian, Spanish, and African cuisines, with slight Arab influence in some regions and it's absolutely delicious!

What To Serve With Sudado De Pollo?

I like to serve this Colombian classic as the natives do: with white rice (Jasmine or Basmati are the best) and avocado slices. But it's also great with crusty bread, pasta, or mashed potatoes.

You could add a generous dollop of sour cream on the top, or leave that out if you want to keep the calories down!

Chicken drumsticks in a flavorful sauce, with rice and avocado slices on the side.

Benefits Of Using Chicken In A Stew:

Chicken is quicker to cook, but it is lower in calories than beef or pork and cheaper too. Win-Win!

Better still, it is suitable for freezing. So why not make double and freeze half? That way you'll have a homemade ready meal for another super busy evening in the future.

How Do I Make This Colombian Dish?

I know I sound like a broken record, but this is an easy recipe to make.

First, we sauté the peppers and onions in oil until the vegetables soften, for a couple of minutes.

Then we add the drumsticks, garlic, tomatoes, salt, and pepper, and cook to brown the meat lightly.

Next, we add potatoes, broth, sazon seasoning, and cilantro.

Lastly, we finish by simmering the stew until potatoes and meat are tender, for about 30 minutes.

Four easy steps to making Colombian Sudado de Pollo dish

Can I Make It In An Instant Pot?

Absolutely! Why not take advantage of your Instant Pot and cook this amazing dish in half the time? For "set it and forget it" kind of meal, see the slow cooker instructions below in the recipe box.

Select the "Sauté" option to pre-heat the Instant Pot. When the word "Hot" appears on display, add the oil, peppers, and onions and sauté until onions are translucent. Press "Cancel" to turn the cooker off.

Add the rest of the ingredients, and close and lock the lid of the Instant Pot. Select "Meat/Stew", "Pressure Cook" or "Manual" and set the timer (+/- button) to 15 minutes.

When time is up, open the lid using Quick Release (press "Cancel" and then turn the steam release handle on the lid to the "Venting" position.)

Overhead view of the dish with chicken stew, a bowl of wite rice, and a small bowl with svocado on the white wooden background.

Recipe Notes/Expert Tips:

This Colombian Chicken Stew will be perfectly cooked and delicious after 30 minutes. Still, you can cook it for up to 90 minutes - longer cooking time will result in a more concentrated and developed flavor.

You can replace the broth (stock) with water and chicken bouillon.

Use boneless, skinless chicken thighs instead of drumsticks. If you prefer, keep the skin on. You can also use chicken breast, but dark meat is more flavorful.

Add more stock or water if it gets too dry. Alternatively, cook uncovered for 10-15 min longer if it's too watery.

You could also transfer your dish to the oven and cook on 375F for 30-45 minutes instead of the stovetop. Make sure to use a Dutch oven, cast-iron, or another oven-proof dish.

This stew is suitable for freezing.

Close up of the chicken dish showing the dish being served.

Colombian Chicken Stew - Sudado de Pollo

This Colombian chicken stew takes 30 minutes, but it tastes like it's been simmering for hours. Serve over white rice or with homemade crusty bread.

Course: Main CourseCuisine: Colombian Prep Time: 15 minutesCook Time: 30 minutesTotal Time: 45 minutes Servings: 4 servings Calories: 401kcal

Equipment

Dutch oven or a skillet with a lid

Kitchen knife

Cutting board

Ingredients

- 1 tablespoon vegetable oil
- ½ cup chopped red bell pepper
- 1 small onion chopped

- 8 chicken drumsticks skinless
- 2 garlic cloves minced
- 3 medium tomatoes chopped
- ¼ teaspoon salt
- ¼ teaspoon pepper
- 1 pound baby potatoes cut in half
- 2 cups chicken broth
- 1 tablespoon sazon goya con azafran
- ¼ teaspoon cumin powder
- ¼ cup chopped fresh cilantro plus more for garnishing
- Avocado for serving optional

Instructions

1. In a Dutch oven or large cast-iron skillet, heat the 1 tablespoon oil over medium heat. Add ½ cup chopped red pepper and one chopped onion; sauté until onions are translucent, about 3-4 minutes.

2. Add 8 skinless chicken drumsticks, 2 minced garlic cloves, 3 chopped tomatoes, and season with ¼ tsp of

each salt and pepper. Cook until lightly browned, often stirring, about 4 minutes.

3. Add 1 lb baby potatoes, 2 cups chicken broth, 1 tbsp Sazon seasoning, ¼ tsp cumin, and ¼ cup chopped cilantro.

4. Bring the stew to a boil, reduce the heat to medium-low, partially cover, and simmer for 30 minutes or until potatoes are tender. Sprinkle with fresh cilantro and serve with avocado slices over rice.

Notes

This Colombian Chicken Stew will be perfectly cooked and delicious after 30 minutes. Still, you can cook it for up to 90 minutes - longer cooking time will result in a more concentrated and developed flavor.

You can replace the chicken broth (stock) with water and chicken bouillon.

Use boneless, skinless chicken thighs instead of drumsticks. If you prefer, keep the skin on. You can also use chicken breast, but dark meat is more flavorful.

Add more stock or water if it gets too dry. Alternatively, cook uncovered for 10-15 min longer if it's too watery.

This stew can also be cooked in a slow cooker: add all ingredients to your slow cooker and cook for 3 hours on high or 6 hours on low.

Want to make it in your IP? Check out the instructions in the post above.

You could also transfer your dish to the oven and cook on 375F for 30-45 minutes. Make sure to use a Dutch oven, cast-iron, or another oven-proof dish.

This stew is suitable for freezing.

Nutrition information is approximate and meant as a guideline only.

Nutrition

Calories: 401kcal | Carbohydrates: 28g | Protein: 31g | Fat: 18g | Saturated Fat: 7g | Cholesterol: 139mg | Sodium: 747mg | Potassium: 1207mg | Fiber: 4g | Sugar: 5g | Vitamin A: 1489IU | Vitamin C: 70mg | Calcium: 54mg | Iron: 3mg

Aguacate Relleno de Atún (Tuna Stuffed Avocado)

Stuffed avocados are a popular appetizer in Colombia and other parts of Latin America. We stuffed them with shrimp, fish, chicken, crab or tuna salad in Colombia.

This Aguacate Relleno de Atún (Tuna Stuffed Avocado) recipe is very easy to make and a fantastic lunch, appetizer or summer dinner. The avocados are cut in halves and stuffed with tuna, peas, carrots, tomato, parsley, cilantro, mayo, hot sauce and ketchup.

Ingredients:

- 2 cans of good quality tuna fish
- 1/4 cup grated white onion
- 2 tablespoon finely chopped red onion
- 1/4 cup cooked peas
- 1/4 cup cooked and diced carrots
- 1/2 tomato, diced
- 1/4 cup of ketchup

- 1/4 cup of mayonnaise
- 1/2 teaspoon hot sauce
- 2 tablespoons chopped parsley
- 2 tablespoons chopped cilantro
- 6 ripe but firm avocados
- Juice of 2 limes
- Salt and pepper to taste

Directions

1. Combine the tuna, onions,red onion, peas, carrots, tomato, ketchup, mayo, hot sauce, parsley, cilantro and juice of 1 lime. Mix all the ingredients and add salt and pepper to your taste.
2. Cut the avocados lengthwise, remove the seed and, drizzle lime juice to prevent them from darkening.
3. Place the avocados halves on a serving plate. Fill the avocados with the tuna mixture and sprinkle with chopped cilantro or parsley. Serve immediately.

27-Ingredient Panzanella Antipasta

1. arugula

2. radicchio

3. endive

4. cucumber

5. olives

6. fennel

7. parsley

8. basil

9. French stringbeans

10. red onion

11. marinated artichoke hearts

12. capers

13. olives

14. sweet roasted pepper

15. tomato

16. radish

17. garlic

18. toasted bread croutons

19. sopressata (Italian dry-cured salami)

20. bocaccini (mozzarella balls)

21. sun-dried tomato

22. olive oil

23. balsamic vinegar

24. parmigiana

25. salt

26. fresh ground black pepper

27. oregano

Ají de Huevo Colombiano (Colombian Egg Ají)

Ingredients:

- 7 large eggs
- 3 tablespoons white vinegar
- 3 tablespoons lemon juice
- 1/2 teaspoon dried chili flakes or to your taste
- Salt and pepper to your taste
- 1/4 teaspoon sugar
- 1/4 cup finely chopped cilantro
- 2 tablespoons finely chopped fresh parsley leaves

Instructions

1. Place the eggs in a pan in a single layer, and fill the pan with enough cold water so that it covers the eggs by about an inch. Bring to a boil over high heat, then remove the pan from the heat, cover, and let stand for 10 minutes.

2. Carefully pour out the hot water; place the pan in the sink and run cold water over the eggs until the pan is lukewarm, 1 to 2 minutes. Drain and refill with cold water, let stand until the eggs are room temperature, about 10 minutes.

3. Gently crack the eggs all over and peel under running water. Dry the eggs, then chop into small pieces.

4. In a bowl, whisk the vinegar, lemon juice, hot pepper flakes, salt, pepper, and sugar. Add the cilantro, parsley, and mix well. Add the chopped eggs and mix until well combined, taste and and adjust seasoning, if necessary. Serve or refrigerate until ready to use.

Apple and Shrimp Salad with Spicy Nut Dressing

Ingredients

(2 servings)

- One green apple, peeled and diced
- 1/2 cup cucumber, diced

- 1/2 pound of cooked shrimp, cut into bite size pieces
- 3/4 cup almonds
- 1/4 cup red onion, finely chopped
- 1/4 cup chopped fresh cilantro leaves, plus more for garnish
- 1/2 cup grape tomatoes, halved
- Salt and pepper, to taste
- 3 bacon strips, cooked and diced

Nut Dressing

- 3 tablespoons peanut butter
- 1 tablespoon fresh lime juice
- 1 tablespoon white vinegar
- 1 tablespoon water
- 1/2 jalapeño pepper, finely chopped
- Salt and pepper, to taste

Directions

1. In a small bowl mix all the dressing ingredients and set aside. In a large bowl, toss together the salad ingredients, except the bacon.
2. Drizzle the dressing over the mixture, add the bacon and fresh cilantro, and serve immediately.

Arugula, Corn, Egg and Bean Salad

Ingredients

(4-6 servings)

- 4 cups roasted or grilled corn kernels (4 ears)
- 4 cooked eggs, sliced
- 1 small red onion, thinly sliced
- 1 pin of grape tomatoes
- 4 oz arugula
- 3 cups mixed beans (white, red and garbanzo beans)

Dressing

- Juice of 2 limes
- Juice of 1 lemon

- 3 tablespoons white vinegar
- 3 tablespoons olive oil
- 1/4 teaspoon ground cumin
- 1/4 teaspoon sugar
- Salt and pepper

Directions:

1. Combine all the salad ingredients in a bowl. Add the dressing, then toss and serve.

Arugula Orzo Salad

Ingredients

- 1 pound orzo pasta
- 3 lemons
- Salt
- 1 ½ cup dried cranberries
- 1 cup fresh basil
- 1 ½ cup pine nuts

- ½ teaspoon black pepper
- 4 oz baby arugula
- 2/3 cups olive oil
- 2 cups feta cheese

Directions

2. Bring a large saucepan of lightly salted water to a boil. Add the orzo and cook until tender, but still firm to the bite. Drain the pasta and set aside to cool.
3. Place the arugula, basil, pine nuts, and cranberries in a large salad bowl, mix well and then add the orzo.
4. Mix together the lemon juice and olive oil in a small bowl. Pour the mixture over the salad and mix well.
5. Add the feta cheese and toss together, using 2 forks until well mixed. Keep in the refrigerator until ready to serve.

Avocado Filled with Chicken (Aguacate Relleno de Pollo)

Ingredients

- 2 servings
- 1 avocado, cut lengthwise
- 2 cups cooked chicken, shredded
- 2 tablespoons grated onion
- 1/4 cup chopped fresh cilantro
- 1/4 teaspoon ground cumin
- 1/4 teaspoon paprika
- 1/4 cup crema fresca or creme fraiche
- 1/4 cup mayonnaise
- 1 tablespoon ketchup
- 1 teaspoons fresh lime juice
- Salt and pepper
- 1 small tomato, finely chopped

Directions

1. In a bowl, combine chicken, cumin and paprika.

2. In a small bowl, combine crema fresca, mayonnaise, ketchup, lime juice, salt, and pepper.

3. Add small bowl mixture to chicken mixture, tossing gently to coat. Cover and chill.

4. Fill the avocados with the chicken mixture, top each avocado with tomato and sprinkle with chopped cilantro. Serve immediately.

Made in the USA
Monee, IL
14 March 2023